Summary of

Moonwalking with Einstein

The Art and Science of Remembering Everything

by Joshua Foer

Instaread

Please Note

This is a summary with analysis.

Table of Contents

Overview

Moonwalking with Einstein recounts author Joshua Foer's yearlong journey from participant-journalist covering the national memory championships to becoming the 2006 USA World Memory Champion. Other segments offer a journalistic history of the human relationship with memory, addressing its failings, its successes, and its limitations.

Most people operate according to a series of misconceptions about human memory. Above all, many believe that they have an average brain and are therefore incapable of performing mental feats such as swiftly memorizing a deck of playing cards shuffled into random order. This belief, however, is false. Memory champions are no smarter than anyone else and have unremarkable brains from a biological standpoint. The difference is in how memory champions use their brain. They employ techniques and training to overcome shortcomings that are hard-wired into the human brain anatomy. Even those who appear to possess a photographic memory likely do not and are instead employing other memorization techniques.

Instead of considering impressive feats of memory as reserved for the preternaturally gifted, anyone can learn to train their own mind to excel in this area. Techniques include the time-honored tradition known as the memory palace. This method dates back to ancient Greece and allows the practitioner to convert any information into a spatial memory—the type of information that the human mind recalls best. Other techniques include "chunking," a process by which the person memorizing the information groups large amounts of data into smaller portions and then manages them using familiar mnemonic devices.

Improving one's memory is hard work, plain and simple. There is no shortcut to developing the skills of a mental athlete. Remembering any information, from someone's name at a dinner party to the first thousand digits of π, requires focus, attention, and effort to store the information using a series of acquired techniques.

The notion that anyone can improve their own memory is seductive. If memories make up the fabric of a person's identity, retaining more information might lead to a more enriching life. In the past, great thinkers were expected to memorize and retain volumes of literature, poetry, and philosophy; today, however, most people rely on the fact that answers are just a Google search away. Although convenient, reliance on externalized memory has weakened people's ability to remember anything for themselves.

Moonwalking with Einstein was first published in 2011.

Important People

Joshua Foer is a journalist and the author of *Moonwalking with Einstein*.

Anthony "Tony" Buzan is a British self-help maven who has built a profitable empire from teaching memorization techniques. He is also the founder of the World Memory Championship.

Ben Pridmore was the reigning world memory champion in 2004 whose story inspired Foer to pursue his research into mental athletes.

Ed Cooke is a British mental athlete who trained and mentored the author in memory techniques.

Alexander Luria (1902-1977) was a Russian psychologist who studied a journalist, known only as S, who had seemingly infinite capacity for memorization.

K. Anders Ericsson is a professor of psychology at Florida State University. He has written extensively on what makes a person an expert and on the type of effort required to develop expertise in a given area.

Daniel Tammet is a self-proclaimed savant with extraordinary mental abilities. Foer casts doubt on the veracity of his claims by proving that many of his mental talents can be achieved by employing memory-building techniques.

Laurence Kim Peek (1951-2009) was a rare example of a savant with extraordinary mental capacity due to brain damage sustained in his early years. He was the inspiration for the movie *Rain Main* (1988).

Key Takeaways

1. Anyone can train their memory to perform feats that appear impossible for an average mind.

2. Most people never develop an exceptional memory because their skills are sufficient for everyday life and they see no benefits to improving them.

3. The rise of the printing press contributed to the decline of the art of memorization.

4. The modern American education system and Western society as a whole have come to devalue memorization.

5. The so-called memory palace technique is the most famous and effective method of memorization employed by mental athletes.

6. Elaborative encoding is the process of taking something unmemorable and turning it into a vivid, mental image that is unforgettable.

7. The existence of photographic memory has not been proven.

8. Attention is a major component of memorization.

Thank you for purchasing this Instaread book

Download the Instaread mobile app to get unlimited text & audio summaries of bestselling books.

Visit Instaread.co
to learn more.

Analysis

Key Takeaway 1

Anyone can train their memory to perform feats that appear impossible for an average mind.

Analysis

Winners of memory competitions have average memories. They are not savants or geniuses. They are simply well-trained. When the brains of mental athletes are studied, they are found to have no exceptional structural differences from the brains of other people. However, memory champions do use their brains differently.

Albert Einstein is the most famous example of how some people's exemplary mental capabilities are not necessarily indicative of a remarkable brain structure. Most famously, studies of Einstein's brain have shown that while his anatomy had some differences from a typical brain, it was impossible for researchers to be sure whether or not those differences were the reason for his genius or the product of his devotion to learning. Einstein could have been born with a perfectly normal brain that developed structural changes through his life's work. [1] The determinist belief that people with exceptional cerebral capabilities must have been born with exceptional or special brain physiognomy is therefore misguided, however widespread.

Key Takeaway 2

Most people never develop an exceptional memory because their skills are sufficient for everyday life and they see no benefits to improving them.

Analysis

Those who develop superior skills are people who engage in "deliberate practice," a term developed by Anders Ericsson to describe a rigorous form of skill development. Those who languish on the "OK Plateau" operate on autopilot instead of consciously developing a skill and learning from failure.

For example, a very talented amateur chef likely has a stable of recipes that he returns to with great frequency and which never fail to please his family and friends. Perhaps he prefers to cook mostly Italian food because his grandmother was from Tuscany and he grew up eating Italian cuisine. For this chef, making spaghetti Bolognese might be something he could do blindfolded. While the results are admirable, cooking may not require much conscious thought and effort on his part. But what if this amateur chef wanted to enter the competitive world of professional cooking? His stable of recipes, while satisfactory, would not make him an expert chef capable of producing a traditional Japanese meal. Instead, he would have to experiment with new techniques, new flavors, and new ingredients, and learn from his failures along the way. This could be an unpleasant and even expensive undertaking for the chef. But in order to rise from the "OK Plateau," he would have to engage his mind actively in his cooking and not rely on skills that have become second nature.

Key Takeaway 3

The rise of the printing press contributed to the decline of the art of memorization.

Analysis

Before the printing press, the written word was hard to come by. In order to return to an idea presented in a text, a person often had to be able to recall it. Even after the invention of the printing press, books were extremely rare and expensive by modern standards. The art of memorization thus remained a highly prized component of Western education. Scholars were expected to memorize classical texts and poetry. Having strong recall of a text was considered demonstrative of a profound engagement with and understanding of the information it contained. In contemporary Western societies, by contrast, externalized memory has become a part of daily reality. Physical and digital repositories of information are assumed to preserve all knowledge and prevent the social collapse that would result from a massive loss of human knowledge.

The decline of education in Europe during the Middle Ages offers an example of the social perils of relying on external memory rather than learned cultural memory that is taught by one generation to the next. Much of the population across Europe remained illiterate during the Middle Ages. The canon of classical texts was largely forgotten due to the fact that these texts were not translated into vernacular languages from their original Greek or Latin. Very few people had the means and opportunity to learn Greek or Latin in the Middle Ages, which meant almost no one could read these foundational texts on medicine, science, art, and philosophy. As a result, society and technology faltered and lost ground from prior achievements of the Roman Empire. [2] One significant example would be the use of concrete as a building material. The great buildings of the Roman Empire, some of which still stand today, showed a mastery of engineering and concrete production processes that were lost during the Middle Ages. The Roman Colosseum is a well-known example. It wasn't until the fifteenth century that manuscripts from ancient Rome detailing concrete production were rediscovered. Only then did concrete begin to reemerge as a crucial building material in Europe. [3]

Key Takeaway 4

The modern American education system and Western society as a whole have come to devalue memorization.

Analysis

Memorization and creativity go hand-in-hand. Just as creative thought helps to retain memories, memorization aids the development of creative concepts and ideas. Yet memorization is regarded as inhibiting to creative, independent thought. Memorization has thus largely disappeared from the pedagogy of most Western schools. Western society as a whole has come to devalue memorization as modern technologies such as smartphones and even Google have made it possible to perform routine tasks without relying on memory or spending the thousands of hours required to train it to retain vast amounts of information.

With increased access to Google and other Internet search and storage devices, consumers have become increasingly reliant on computers and the Internet for information that, in the past, they would have needed to remember. While most people in the late twentieth century would have had many of their friends' and relatives' phone numbers memorized, almost no one with a cellphone sees the need for memorizing telephone numbers. A 2011 Columbia University study demonstrated that people do not actively attempt to retain certain information when they know that they will have easy access to it any time in the future. However, given the human brain's preference for spatial memory, researchers found that people were better at recalling where information could be accessed than they were at recalling the information itself. [4]

Key Takeaway 5

The so-called memory palace technique is the most famous and effective method of memorization employed by mental athletes.

Analysis

The human mind does not remember all types of information equally. Spatial information is the easiest for the human mind to retain thanks to human evolution from hunting and gathering societies in which it was important to remember where food and water resources were but not lists of names or numbers. In recognition of this evolutionary preference for spatial information, the memory palace technique organizes information by having memorizers create mental images of the things they are trying to remember and put them at locations in a familiar place.

The human spatial memory has two reference points that are used to retain and recall information across a wide variety of locations. The first is defined by the object's position in relation to the observer. The second is defined by the object's relative position to other objects. Both of these references are needed in order to create a mental map. [5] For example, your mind might map both where your light switch is in relation to your door and in relation to you, enabling you to find it easily in the dark. The memory palace is able to exploit both of these reference points by taking the memorizer on a subjective journey through a familiar space.

Key Takeaway 6

Elaborative encoding is the process of taking something unmemorable and turning it into a vivid, mental image that is unforgettable.

Analysis

Racy or violent images are often more memorable than things you might encounter on any given day. If a man constantly forgets his keys when he leaves the house, he may find it helpful to create a mental image of his keys in a bloody sword fight blocking his way to the door. Or perhaps a frequent traveler is worried that she will forget where she parked her car at the airport when she returns from vacation. She may observe that her car is on the fourth floor of the west parking garage. Recalling the number "four" and the direction "west" might be tricky as neither are very memorable. However, if she imagines the number four in full cowboy regalia, stomping into a saloon, guns drawn, in the Wild West, she may be better able to remember where she parked when she returns from her trip. Such vivid mental images take commonplace or abstract concepts and make them memorable.

Since developing these striking images is so important, creativity is an essential tool in developing memorization skills. Another technique of elaborative encoding is the Person-Action-Object (PAO) method in which mental athletes prepare by creating singular images for every number that they can call upon whenever they need to memorize a number. Suppose the number one is Madonna dancing on a cupcake, the number two is a beaver eating a hotdog. When a long series of numbers is broken into groups of two digits, the mental athlete can recall where each number is in a sequence at all times by combining these images. If the number is 12, it will be Madonna dancing on a hotdog. The first digit takes the number's person (P) and action (A) and the second takes on its object (O). Thus, creative combinations such as "moonwalking with Einstein" are often what populate the mental athlete's imaging.

Key Takeaway 7

The existence of photographic memory has not been proven.

Analysis

Human memories are made up of neurological connections and associations. Increasing the strength of those connections is the key to improving memory. While some people excel at doing this, there are no well-proven instances of photographic memory documented by science. The notion of the savant is also flawed. In most cases, people who present with savant-like abilities have damage to the brain's left hemisphere which allows the right hemisphere to become dominant.

While science has yet to discover a reliable instance of a photographic memory, one study in particular further suggests its impossibility. In this study, researchers found that people do not store memories of photographs the same way that they remember the pictures themselves. In short, if a photographic memory were possible, the process of recalling a memory would mirror the mental process of recalling an actual photograph. [6] However, this study found that the human mind does not recall photographs in the same way it retains real-live images.

Key Takeaway 8

Attention is a major component of memorization.

Analysis

Most people forget the names of new acquaintances because they're simply not paying enough attention when they're being introduced. A mental athlete or a person developing memory skills will apply great focus at the moment that new information is being introduced in order to retain it, often employing a mnemonic device to do so.

Attention is such an important part of retaining memories that when studying learning disabilities, such as ADHD, specialists and researchers have focused on the role of working memory. Not surprisingly, studies found ADHD patients to have significantly impaired working memories. [7] Even in studies that focused on subjects who do not present with ADHD or a similar disorder, researchers have found that a lack of attention or even an outright distraction has a clearly negative impact on memory and recall. [8]

Author's Style

Joshua Foer's style changes throughout the book. While at some points he takes the stance of a journalist, at others he becomes inextricably tied to his subject and deeply invested in his own personal road to becoming a memory champion. He frequently asserts that he has an average memory and shares his insecurities as he prepares for the memory championship. Even after winning the championship, however, he points out that his functional memory for everyday tasks remains average at best. He reflects on one particular occasion after his win: while on the subway home from a dinner with his friends, he realizes he forgot that he had driven to the restaurant in the first place. He also asserts that memory work is challenging even for an expert. He explains that he reverts to using crutches like his phone or a Post-It note to remember phone numbers and other details in spite of all the skills he's gained.

Author's Perspective

Joshua Foer began his journey into understanding the art of memorization as a spectator when he covered the 2005 USA Memory Championship for *Slate*. However, his journalistic interest quickly became a personal obsession when his interviews with competitors revealed time and again that they have average memories and that anyone can excel in memory competitions with proper training. Foer's perspective then becomes that of a competitor in training. He bonds with his fellow mental athletes and becomes such a significant part of their lives that they induct him into their secret society. Most poignantly, his perspective diverges so starkly from that of an unattached journalist-observer that at one point, while inebriated at a party with his fellow memory champions, he hands over his reporter's notebook to a third party to take notes for him.

Nevertheless, Foer remains skeptical of the utility of mastering memory techniques. He makes it clear that he still struggles to remember basic information just like anyone else despite his national memory championship.

~~~~ END OF INSTAREAD ~~~~

Thank you for purchasing this Instaread book

**Download the Instaread mobile app to get
unlimited text & audio summaries
of bestselling books.**

Visit Instaread.co
to learn more.

References

1. Kremer, William. "The strange afterlife of Einstein's brain." *BBC News*. April 18, 2015. Accessed June 2, 2016. http://www.bbc.com/news/magazine-32354300

2. Rubenstein, Richard E. *Aristotle's Children: How Christians, Muslims, and Jews Rediscovered Ancient Wisdom and Illuminated the Dark Ages*. Orlando: Harcourt, 2003.

3. Guedes, Pedro. *The Macmillan Encyclopedia of Architecture and Technological Change*. London: Macmillan, 1979.

4. Sparrow, Betsy, et al. "Google Effects on Memory: Cognitive Consequences of Having Information at Our Fingertips." *Science* 333, no. 6043 (August 5, 2011): 776-78. Accessed June 2, 2016. http://science.sciencemag.org/content/333/6043/776

5. Mehta, Mitul A. "Spatial Memory in Humans." *Encyclopedia of Psychopharmacology*, 2014, 1-6. Accessed June 2, 2016. http://link.springer.com/referenceworkentry/10.1007%2F978-3-642-27772-6_355-2

6. Varakin, D. Alexander, and Lester Loschky. "Object appearance and picture-specific viewpoint are not integrated in long-term memory."

The Quarterly Journal of Experimental Psychology 63, no. 6 (May 24, 2010): 1181-200. Accessed June 2, 2016. http://www.k-state.edu/psych/vcl/documents/Varakin_Loschky_2010.pdf

7. Lenartowicz, Agatha, et al. "Electroencephalography Correlates of Spatial Working Memory Deficits in Attention-Deficit/Hyperactivity Disorder: Vigilance, Encoding, and Maintenance." *Journal of Neuroscience* 34, no. 4 (January 22, 2014): 1171-182. Accessed June 2, 2016. http://www.jneurosci.org/content/34/4/1171.full

8. Beaman, C. Philip, et al. "The effects of distraction on metacognition and metacognition on distraction: Evidence from recognition memory." *Frontiers in Psychology* 5 (May 14, 2014). Accessed June 2, 2016. http://www.ncbi.nlm.nih.gov/pubmed/24860543